No Turning Back

a salvation story of India

Adapted from Gunti Family recollections

Illustrated by Kalidas "Das" Thadi

Helping Children See Jesus

biblevisuals.org

Our mission: To produce and provide visualized curriculum to ministry partners worldwide

Bible Visuals International exists to produce curriculum that is gospel-focused, scripturally sound and visually excellent and to provide it to our ministry partners worldwide in ways that are affordable, accessible and adaptable to their needs.

Our vision: Helping Children See Jesus

Bible Visuals International envisions that all children would have the opportunity to trust Jesus Christ as their Savior and to experience God's redemptive power in their lives.

BVI is a 501(c)(3) charity organization. We rely on the support of ministry partners like you to help us in our mission. If you would like to learn more, please visit our website at **biblevisuals.org**.

Scan the QR code to find more information and videos related to this story.

Page layout & design: Elly Kalagayan & Jeff Kilcup

PO Box 153, Akron, PA 17501-0153
717.859.1131

biblevisuals.org

ISBN 978-1-64104-269-7

No Turning Back

a salvation story of India

A Dangerous Place

Have you ever visited a place and loved it so much that you didn't want to leave? Maybe it was just that beautiful or that much fun or maybe you didn't want to leave because of who you were with in that place. In our mission story we're going to learn that there is someone who is so good and great and who changes us so much on the inside that we never want to turn away from following Him, no matter the cost.

Have you been to India? India is a big country in Southeast Asia. There are so many people who live there that it has the largest population in the world! While there are Christians who live there now, many people in India do not know about Jesus and His love. Instead they worship false gods that have no power. Many poor people there hope that these gods will help them.

This true story takes place many years ago for one troubled couple.

Venkanna slashed at the brush in front of him with his long-bladed knife. It was the time of monsoons in India and the clouds above him were darkening. "We may have to hunt for some shelter," he told his wife, Pochamma. A stubborn branch didn't snap with the first slash of his knife, so he hacked at it again. When it landed on the ground, he bent over and shoved it to one side. "Up there! Look!" he pointed his hand towards a grove of slender, yet tall trees growing in a clump. "Just perfect for the poles we need for the roof."

The two fought their way up the slope of the hill.

The Hindu couple had set out early that morning to collect the poles they needed for their new house. They had to walk for two hours before they finally reached this rough, rocky hillside, densely covered with brush and trees. Then, Venkanna had to make a path as they left the already harvested area for better and taller trees.

"Enough for the entire roof," Pochamma said, her eyes smiling with delight.

They were not going to make a big house. Roughly 15 feet by 20 feet, their new home would be crude and small, but this was how most of the people in India lived in the 1900s. The Gunti couple was no different.

Venkanna drank from the pottery jug, but only a little. That jug of water would have to last both of them the entire day, for they did not know of any well nearby. Water was a precious commodity and cherished carefully.

Pochamma was already walking among the slender trees, delighting in their straight trunks. Sure, they would eventually bow beneath the weight of the thatch, but that didn't matter. They would be plenty strong enough to support their roof above their heads. A roof needed only to be able to shield them from the rains and give them shade during the hot summer when the temperatures soared way above one hundred degrees.

Venkanna pulled his axe from the rope belt he had tied around his waist and began chopping at the first tree. As soon as he had felled it, Pochamma began trimming the branches off. Deftly, she slashed at the thin horizontal branches and then dragged the pole to one side.

The Indian couple worked together in the clammy weather. They were used to the weather, though. Both of them had lived in the area just outside Hyderabad in central India all their lives, and as far as they knew, so had their ancestors.

When the first rain drops spattered on them, the two kept on working. They were not afraid of getting wet.

Then, it began raining harder.

"We had better seek shelter!" Venkanna yelled at his wife, speaking above the sound of the rain all around them. "This will be a deluge."

Monsoon rains can be heavy, and even though this was only the beginning of the rainy season, sometimes the downpours lasted a long time. Pochamma straightened herself up from her task and tried to wipe the rain from her eyes. "There!" she yelled, pointing to an outcrop of rocks on the hillside up the slope from where they were working.

Venkanna nodded and the two scrambled up, gasping as the rain drenched their faces. They reached the area just below the jutting rock cliff above them and immediately went underneath the shelter and sighed, relieved to be out of the driving rain. Their bare feet got covered with the dry soil that turned rapidly to mud as the water dripped off their clothes and puddled beneath them. Pochamma used her sari and wiped her face and hair. She sighed and sat down on a round rock. In front of them, the water poured down over the rock and splashed the boulders that formed a small barrier along the front of the cave.

"Now we can fill the water jug!" Venkanna took the jug and went to the mouth of the cave. He selected a relatively clean stream of water and filled the jug. After the water jug had set for a little while, any debris would settle to the bottom and they could drink the top water.

"There is a hole going under the rocks just over there," he mentioned to his wife, and then wished he wouldn't have, for Pochamma clutched at her throat and looked nervously at where her husband was pointing his finger.

Wild animals and snakes were all around the city of Hyderabad. In fact, one of the reasons the grove of trees they had found was as tall as they had found it was because not many people were brave enough to venture this far into the brush.

Then, the rain poured down even heavier, and a small rivulet formed as it ran down the small incline towards the dark hole.

"I thought the rain would not be this heavy early in the season," Venkanna mused as he stared into the deluge. "I wanted to get all the poles we can carry today and make it productive. If this rain keeps up, we will have to come back more than one more day."

Somehow, Pochamma had been able to keep the naan bread she had wrapped to bring along dry, and the two ate hungrily. It had been a long time since they had eaten curry-flavored rice at daybreak.

Still the rain continued and the two under the sheltering cliff were glad for the rest, yet chaffed with the delay. "I hope we don't have to spend the night here," Venkanna said. "But there is no way we can walk home in this." Sometimes rain storms lasted for hours.

Once more, Pochamma glanced towards the dark hole to the right of where they were sitting.

Suddenly, off to their right, a tawny tiger came bounding out of the rain, his striped fur wet and streaming from the rain. Pochamma gave a stifled cry at the sudden appearance of the giant cat and she shrank against the rock behind her. Venkanna sat motionless as the tiger shook himself like a dog and water drops flew everywhere. Then, the tiger looked with unblinking eyes at the couple, only about fifteen feet away and the terrified couple could see his sides heaving from the dash through the rain for the sheltering rock.

Pochamma felt a scream of terror begin to rise up from deep inside of her and, as though Venkanna sensed what was about to happen, he whispered above the sound of the rain and said, "Don't move and don't scream."

With a great effort, Pochamma stifled the yell and, in spite of her husband's words, felt herself begin to shake in fear.

"Don't look at him in the eyes," Venkanna said, averting his own eyes so he could still see the giant beast but was no longer looking at him directly. "If you need to, close your eyes."

Pochamma did not dare shut her eyes all the way, so she lowered her eyelids and looked through her long black lashes.

The tiger continued to stand motionless, except for the tip of his tail twitching slightly from side to side.

The scene under the rock seemed surreal to the couple, they cowering on the one side of the cave, the rain streaming down in a relentless torrent, and on the opposite side the powerful tiger standing motionless, staring at the couple that had intruded into his domain.

The minutes seemed to drag in tortuously slow ticks as the beast stared at the couple. Then, when he began moving towards the back of the cave, Pochamma had another panic attack and held her breath.

At the edge of the hole, the tiger stopped, turned his massive head towards the couple, twitched his tail for several seconds, then disappeared into the blackness.

There was no need for communication between the terrified couple. Never mind the rain! They fled down the slope of the hill as fast as they could go.

When they reached the place where they had cut the poles, Venkanna yelled, “Let’s take these!”

Miraculously, the rain had slackened, and even though Pochamma wanted to continue their flight she let reason rule and they tied the five poles together hastily. With Venkanna leading the way and Pochamma taking the rear, they began their slippery descent downhill.

Venkanna kept up a fairly brisk pace and Pochamma used all of her strength to keep up. She did not dare turn her head to check the path behind them, for she knew if she did, she would be dragged by the forward motion of her husband carrying the front end of the poles.

It was almost dark by the time the couple finally reached their crude hut at the edge of the city. The dirt path between the rough huts was sloppy with mud and even though the rain had almost completely stopped, everything was drenched and muddy streams of water ran everywhere.

Rain had leaked through the roof during the downpour and Pochamma was dismayed to find her meager pile of clothes drenched. She strung the clothes on a line inside of their leaky hut and then, even though she was so tired and exhausted from the long day, she lit the charcoal brazier, moved it to the front of their dark hut beneath the overhang, and cooked a pot of rice. Her nerves still quivered from her fright and the hurried flight down the mountainside. She was so exhausted by the time supper was over that she could barely move. When she found that the roof had leaked in a new spot and soaked the mat where they slept, she hardly cared and lay down anyway, too tired to move.

Chapter Conclusion

Venkanna and Pochamma experienced a very scary situation, didn't they? After they picked up their poles, do you think they thought of returning to those rocks? Of course not! There was a dangerous tiger there. That would be foolish to go back to such a place. But, did you know there was something more dangerous that Venkanna and Pochamma needed to turn away from? It was their sin against the Creator God. Our sin is our disobedience against God and what He says is right and good. Because of our sin against God, we rightly deserve judgment from Him.

Sin is seen in the thoughts we think, the words we speak and the things we do. Our sin isn't just a little problem. It runs right down to the core of who we are as humans. We must turn away from that sin and trust in the one who can save us from it: Jesus, the Son of God. But, first we need help to see that we are sinners against God. That's why God in love has given us His Word, the Bible.

It's also why Christians go around the world to share the Bible and the good news of Jesus with others. We often call those people missionaries. Venkanna and Pochamma needed someone to share the Word of God with them so that they might turn from sin and trust in Jesus.

Looking for Hope

Venkanna led the way out of the burial plot. Two professional male mourners followed him, and after Venkanna gave them each a coin, they disappeared. The sad man left the cemetery, each tiny grave marked by a simple stone or a piece of wood. Infant corpses were not cremated, as were the bodies of adults, and there was not the usual gathering of the villagers afterwards.

Pochamma was not with him. She was back in their new hut, built with the poles they had gotten from "Tiger" mountain, as they now called that hill. Venkanna's wife was recovering from delivering the stillborn baby. A boy, it had been.

This was the fourth infant Venkanna had to bury. None of the babies had survived.

As the burdened man passed a roadside shrine, he hesitated, then walked right on past. Bringing offerings to the Hindu gods had not done any good before, and he had lost faith anything or anyone could help them now.

The couple was already in their mid-thirties. They desperately wanted children.

Venkanna's work as a sorghum farmer barely provided food for their own table, let alone any to sell at the marketplace. Yet, from out of his meager savings, the couple had paid hard-earned rupees to the priests at the shrines and temples and asked for prayers for a living child. Just let them at least have one child!

Venkanna tried not to think of the years that stretched out ahead of them. He tried to dismiss the dismal picture of he and Pochamma becoming old, childless. It was not a pleasant thing to think about.

They had seen other childless couples in their old age. Finally, too feeble to fend for themselves, many times they starved to death if no one had mercy on them and fed them. Even so, hardly any neighbor would or could sufficiently feed someone not related to them.

Thus, as the distraught man walked away from the burial ground where infants were buried, his heart was heavy. Yama, the god of death, had gotten another victim.

Ahead, he saw a group of people gathered in the middle of the street in their Dalit neighborhood. The Dalit, his own caste, lived in miserable huts until the wooden poles rotted or got riddled with insects and they had to rebuild, as Venkanna had done.

The Dalit, the poorest caste in all of India, lived most of their lives in abject poverty and even the very name, Dalit, means crushed or broken to pieces. Often called the "untouchables" by the other castes, they were considered the scum of society.

Then, Venkanna saw an amazing sight! A foreigner, a white man was in their slums! Venkanna pressed closer and looked curiously at the middle-aged man.

"I come to tell you of the living God," the white man said, and Venkanna almost gasped. Astonished, his mouth hung open in surprise, for this white man spoke in Telugu, the local dialect. How odd it was to hear his own language coming from a foreigner.

Venkanna was well aware of the presence of the British in India, for Great Britain's presence was everywhere in what they considered their colony. The higher castes were continually chafing under foreign rule, but for a Dalit such as himself, he hardly ever thought much about politics. He was too busy trying to make a living and providing enough nourishment for Pochamma so they could have a living child.

Then, Venkanna perked up. Another god?

"God has given His own son, Jesus Christ, to the world in order that all people who believe in Him should be saved," the man went on, turning his eyes from man to man.

"God had a son?" one of the men burst out.

The man nodded, "Yes, his name is Jesus." Then he smiled at the group. "Come to Narrow Street tomorrow night and I will tell you more about Jesus. I want you to understand the way of life - of eternal life. Jesus is the best gift God has ever given to the world."

"What is your name?" another curious man asked.

"Mr. Parker. I am from Canada, and I have come to your country to tell you the good news God has for you." Again, he smiled at the group of men. Then, he turned to leave and the group respectfully opened up a way for him to pass without touching them.

"Sir!" Venkanna could not contain himself, "This god, this Jesus," he hesitated over the strange name, "is he powerful?"

"Oh yes," Mr. Parker answered, nodding. "He is as powerful as God, the Creator of heaven and earth. He is the Son of God."

What was it that made the words burn themselves into the heart of this poverty stricken man? How was it possible for a spark to be ignited at the short, but powerful mention of Jesus? Venkanna himself did not know.

Yet, such an impact did the stranger's words make for him that, as soon as he reached his small hut, he spoke to Pochamma.

"On the way home from the cemetery," he told his wife, who was lying on her blanket on the floor, "an amazing thing happened. More than one thing."

After he told her about the meeting, the couple was silent. Then Pochamma said, "He spoke to you? But we are Dalit!"

"That is the amazing thing," Venkanna said slowly, "He talked as though we were not untouchable. He spoke Telugu and understood our words."

"And he came here? To the slums?" Pochamma said incredulously. "No foreigner comes here!"

"And," Venkanna said, "He talked about a Son of God. I find the words burning in here," and he placed his hand over his heart.

Pochamma said nothing but sighed and closed her eyes. "Can you give me water?"

"I have to go draw more," her husband told her as he checked the water jug.

"Oh!" Pochamma wailed, "Death will take me, too, if I have to wait for the half hour to drink. I feel so hot!"

"I will go beg from a neighbor," Venkanna said quickly and left the hut.

"Please, honored mother," Venkanna said to an elderly woman two huts down from theirs, "my wife has just given birth and we are out of water. May I please have some of yours? I will bring back a pail from the well with water for you."

The old woman's eyes narrowed shrewdly, "How will I know if you will? What can you give me for payment?"

Venkanna shook his head, "I am poor. I have nothing."

"Give me your shirt," the old woman said with a shake of her head. "I have to have a token of security."

Without another word, Venkanna took off his shirt. The hot sun would burn into his skin but he was desperate. He put both hands together and bowed as the old woman went inside and gave him a small pottery cup half full of the precious liquid.

Then, Venkanna hurried and lifted the cup to his wife's lips. "I will have to hurry now to get fresh jugs of water for us and the neighbor woman."

The distance to the well took all of the fifteen minutes Venkanna knew it would. Then, he had to wait his turn as the line ahead of him drew water up from the hand dug well. Finally, with a bucket in each hand, the hot and sweating man made his way back carefully to his house and gave his ill wife a long and refreshing drink. Then, he went to retrieve his shirt.

"What shirt?" the old woman said with disdain. "I have no shirt."

Venkanna did not argue. He sighed in resignation and returned home. Now, he was the owner of just one shirt, and that one had holes, for he had been wearing the better of the two for the burial of his son.

He entered their hut and stared at his wife. Pochamma lay still and quiet and before his eyes adjusted to the dark inside of the hut, Venkanna felt fear clutch his heart. Was his wife still breathing?

Then, he saw the slight rise and fall of her chest as she lay in a stupor. The heat outside intensified and the air was stifling inside the mud brick house. But Venkanna did not think about the heat. He was used to that. He did, however, think about the stranger, Mr. Parker, and his unusual appearance. He would go the next day and see what more he could learn about this Jesus. One more god. A powerful one, Mr. Parker had said. Maybe there was hope for them to ask this god for a living baby. He did not know where or how he could get the money to pay for more prayers, but he would see. He was getting desperate.

Chapter Conclusion

Where do you look for hope when things are bad in your life? Maybe you just hope that your luck will improve and circumstances will change. Or maybe you hope that you can get a certain thing or influence a certain person or power to make things better. Maybe you think you can just become strong enough to make things better by your own strength.

Aren't you glad that Venkanna has started to learn about Jesus? Jesus is God's own Son. The hope that He gives us is not in who we are,

or the things we have,

or where we live,

or what happens in life.

No, He gives us hope in Himself. Through faith in Him and what He has done on the cross, we have our sins forgiven and the promise that when this life is over, we will enjoy God's presence forever! We also have His Spirit to live within us. The Holy Spirit is our comforter and strength in life even if our bad circumstances never change. He is with us and will never leave us. That is real hope.

Will Venkanna and Pochamma find this hope in Jesus? We'll see what happens when Venkanna follows the path leading to Mr. Parker's house.

Hope Discovered

Reaching out with determination, Venkanna plucked off the wall of their hut the picture of the Hindu Goddess Kali, one who was claimed to guard death and the afterlife. He placed it on the dirt in front of him. The blue flesh tones of the multi-armed, multi-faced goddess glowed eerily in the semi-darkness. Then, he took down the largest picture of all, Vishnu. A large god, with four arms and standing on a snake, Vishnu was considered to have been reincarnated nine times and still had one more life before reaching a certain state of perfection. Claims were that several of his recycled lives were spent as animals, perhaps one of them as a sacred cow. The Preserver was the Hindu meaning of Vishnu.

But Venkanna did not hesitate.

"What are you doing?" Pochamma asked from her mat. Her brows were furrowed in concern as she watched her husband remove the religious symbols.

"I want to make room for the new god. For Jesus," Venkanna said. "Mr. Parker said Jesus is the most powerful god. I will get pictures of his god and put them here. Perhaps this Jesus will not want to share a house with other gods."

"I will keep my holy stone," Pochamma said with determination. "I will not give up my personal god." Like all Hindus, Pochamma held the belief that she had a personal god that was all her own. The more holy a person lived, the more power and the god or goddess was reputed to be. "Even if I am not even close to holy, I don't want to give up my protection." Pochamma rocked back and forth on the floor.

"I am getting desperate! We must somehow find a god that can give us children. Living children," Venkanna said almost bitterly. "All the gods and goddesses that we have given gifts to have not helped! We need a more powerful god!"

"What will you do with those?" Pochamma nodded at the two pictures. "You can sell them," she said hopefully.

Looking around the house, Venkanna picked up both pictures, turned them face down and, pulling the wooden storage box that held their few clothes away from the wall, he put the pictures behind the box and then shoved the box against the wall.

"I am going to get the new god," Venkanna said, and left his hut. Another rain storm was brewing and Venkanna hurried along the muddy road towards the city.

When he reached the river that ran brown and swollen with the torrential downpour from the day before, Venkanna left the road and went down the path to the water. There, he bathed, wanting to purify himself. First from the uncleanness of having buried their infant son, and also in preparation to receive the new god. Marigold and hibiscus flowers floated all around him, placed there by devoted worshippers hoping to gain favor with the gods. Vigorously, Venkanna scrubbed himself with sand, trying to rid his body of any sin. Then, he went back up on the road and hurried on. The wind blew a few spats of rain against his face, but Venkanna just lowered his head and kept on walking swiftly.

Only a handful of men were underneath the roof of the porch where Mr. Parker lived. The one-story concrete house was surrounded by a high fence, but the houseboy opened the gate quickly if anyone approached.

“Come inside,” Mr. Parker said as hc came to his front door. “Too much rain and wind to be outside.”

Venkanna entered the modest house with the rest. The front room was not overly large, but it was twice the size of Venkanna and Pochamma’s entire hut. A doorway leading into a hall led to a kitchen and several bedrooms.

Venkanna sat on the concrete floor with the others. Mr. Parker sat in a chair, a black book in his hand. “Welcome,” he said with a friendly smile. “We will begin our meeting with prayer.”

At the mention of prayer, the Hindu men all quickly knelt, their heads touching the floor, their hands clasped together in front of their heads. Mr. Parker knelt beside his chair.

Listening intently to Mr. Parker's prayer, Venkanna was amazed as the man spoke plainly and even with boldness to his god. Instead of merely petitioning God for needs he had, Mr. Parker thanked God for answers to prayers and for allowing the men to come and learn more about the way of life. Every prayer Venkanna had ever prayed had been to ask for favor and material blessing in some way.

After the prayer, the men settled themselves on the floor, their knees spread out in front, their feet tucked underneath them. “I will begin telling you the story of Jesus,” Mr. Parker began. “Even at the beginning of Creation, when God created the earth, the heavens, the animals, the plants and all living things, and then finally man - Jesus, the Son of God was already present.”

Venkanna held the common belief that many Hindus accepted that Vishnu suddenly existed and then created Brahmin so the second god could create the world.

As though Mr. Parker knew what he was thinking, he said, “God always existed and He created everything by just speaking. Thus, the world came into existence as we know it.” Then, Mr. Parker went right into the story of the first man and woman. He told the listening men about Adam and Eve, and when he came to the part of the snake, Venkanna listened keenly. He remembered the picture of Vishnu he had taken off the wall. Was Vishnu the same as the God Mr. Parker was talking about? Maybe he would put the picture back on the wall.

“Even though there are many gods in your country, the Bible,” Mr. Parker held up the black book, “teaches there is but one God, the Lord God Jehovah.” Then Mr. Parker talked briefly about the time after the creation and spoke of how the people had many wars and troubles and how prophets preached that a king would some day come into the world.

“That king is Jesus Christ, the Son of God,” Mr. Parker told the listeners simply. “God sent Jesus into the world, born of a young girl by the power of the Holy Spirit.” He told them about the birth of Jesus and Venkanna understood. Gods and goddesses in India often were reputed to have strange phenomena occur to them.

Briefly, yet with feeling, Mr. Parker gave the men an overview of the story of Jesus. For two hours he spoke of the miracles Jesus did and of His compassion and love towards the people. Mr. Parker also included the times when the religious rulers were very unhappy about

Jesus and His teachings. He told the men how Jesus prayed in a hillside garden, and when the soldiers came to Jesus and arrested him, Venkanna felt indignation arise inside of him. He had already grown to admire this man who helped the poor, had compassion on the sick and healed them. Why would the religious leaders be unhappy with such a wonderful man?

"However, as much as our hearts hate the fact that such a man as Jesus was arrested, I will try to explain how God used this very sad episode in the life of Jesus so we can have forgiveness from our sins in this life and eternal life in heaven after we die." Then, Mr. Parker told the attentive men about the trial, the whipping, and the crucifixion of Jesus.

Venkanna felt his heart sink inside of his chest. So, this Jesus was not very powerful after all. He had done nothing to prevent His own death. But then, as Mr. Parker continued the story, Venkanna looked at the white foreigner in disbelief! Jesus rose from the grave by His own power!

"Jesus is alive!" Mr. Parker's voice grew excited. "He is still alive today! The grave could not keep Him, for Jesus has power over death!"

How amazing! That a god would allow himself to be put to death in order to show the world he had power to raise Himself from the dead was very difficult for Venkanna to comprehend. Yet, Mr. Parker did not look like a man who would tell tales. There was a sincerity about him that made it quite easy for the men to believe.

Outside, the wind and rain slowed somewhat as night approached. After Mr. Parker ended his lesson, the houseboy brought a tray of cups and served each man chai! Venkanna sipped the scalding liquid noisily to cool it off before it reached the inside of his mouth. Made with water buffalo milk, it was rich and creamy!

"Come back in three days if you want to hear more," Mr. Parker encouraged the men. "Bring relatives and friends who would like to listen to the story of this wonderful man, Jesus."

Three days later, Venkanna was once again seated in Mr. Parker's house. For two more hours, the group of ten men listened as Mr. Parker told them the stories that Jesus had told His disciples and the crowds who had come to hear Him speak. Again, Venkanna was amazed how much this man Jesus ministered to the poor and the people like his caste, the Dalit. He had a hard time envisioning a man from a ruling class of teachers, like the Brahmins, mingling so freely with the other castes, especially the untouchables like him, a Dalit.

This time, Venkanna lingered after the two-hour session. "Mr. Parker," he said with bowed head and folded hands in front of him to show his recognition of the higher caste of the teacher. " How much does it cost to buy your god? I have saved two rupees, and I want to buy a little god with it. Is it enough? For just a small one?"

When there was no answer, Venkanna allowed himself a quick look at Mr. Parker. What he saw surprised him. It looked as though something had gotten in the man's eye, for his eyes were watering.

"No, Venkanna! My God is not for sale!" Mr. Parker said gently.

"Not for sale, sir?" Venkanna could

not understand. "But I want him. I need him. You see, my wife and I, we have never been able to have any living babies. Four times my wife got pregnant and four times we buried them after they were born. I think your god Jesus is more powerful than the Hindu gods. I can work more and save more money to buy your god. I need him!"

Mr. Parker looked at the earnest face of Venkanna. His heart was moved with compassion by the earnest entreaty and also by the darkness this man was walking in. "You don't understand," he told the man gently. "Jesus is not for sale. He is free! He is not just another god to add to a collection. He is the Son of God! He is alive!"

"How can I know? How can He help me?" Venkanna wondered.

Mr. Parker said nothing for a little while. Then he said, "If you want to and if you can, come tomorrow morning and I will tell you more about Jesus and His wonderful way for us."

Venkanna was silent. He could not afford to stay away from his work. Even the few rupees he did earn were barely enough to buy rice, and yet he did not want to offend this kind foreigner.

"Ahh, I understand," Mr. Parker ascertained. "You must go to your job!"

Venkanna nodded. "I could come in the evening."

Mr. Parker began to shake his head, but then nodded instead. "Come at seven," he said, pushing away his own plans.

Chapter Conclusion

God in His kindness has allowed Venkanna to come and to learn more about Jesus, but Venkanna seems to think that Jesus is just another god among many. Trusting in Jesus as Savior means turning from our old ways too, doesn't it? Will Venkanna be willing to follow Jesus as he learns more, or will he turn back to the ways he has known all his life?

Hope Confessed

Many years ago, when Jesus was on the earth, He taught some things that were hard for people to hear. Some thought of Jesus simply as a good man. They could not accept that He is the Son of God, or that the only way to come to God is through faith in Him alone! After Jesus said these things, the Bible says that many of His followers turned away from following Him. Jesus asked His twelve disciples if they wanted to turn back too.

"... 'Do you want to go away as well?' Simon Peter answered him, 'Lord, to whom shall we go? You have the words of eternal life, and we have believed, and have come to know, that you are the Holy One of God.'" (John 6:68-69)

* * * * *

"He is so friendly!" Venkanna told his wife. "It is hard enough to believe that he allows us Dalit into his house, but then he speaks to us as though we were his equals. I guess foreigners don't understand the caste system."

"No one cares for us," Pochamma said with resignation. "He will turn you away some day. You forget we are untouchables."

"You don't understand," Venkanna replied. "He does not violate our traditions, yet he is kind. He speaks so gently, as though he really cared. I have never seen anyone like him."

"But he didn't let you buy his god," Pochamma reminded him. "He may want to take your soul."

Venkanna did not answer. Was this Mr. Parker up to some devious trick? What could he possibly want from a Dalit? It all seemed so unusual.

"I will go tomorrow night," Venkanna decided. "I will be very observant and watch him closely."

But the next afternoon, the monsoon rains roared in with such power, Venkanna felt he could not make the trek to the foreigner's house. He fretted at the delay and doubts began to plague him. Why would anyone even care about them? Would Mr. Parker change his mind and decide to make him pay a big price to pray to Jesus so they could have a living child? Venkanna had never heard of a priest that didn't charge to intercede to his god on the behalf of those requesting prayers.

Outside, the rain fell in torrents and the wind shook the fragile walls of the hut. For some reason, the storm seemed to echo the turmoil in his brain.

Then, Pochamma gave a shrill cry. "Look! You have put our gods behind the clothes box, and now see! They are ruined!" The distraught woman held up the two pictures that had gotten wet from rain water seeping underneath the walls.

Venkanna shook his head. He looked at the familiar pictures of the Hindu gods. "Throw them away," he said with a sudden decision. "They have not helped us any."

"You blaspheme!" his wife shuddered. "We will all die!" Then she began weeping.

The rain beat down relentlessly on the hundreds of primitive huts as the Dalit village hunkered down to wait until the storm would relent. The untouchables were used to misery and darkness, yet that did not bring any thread of comfort to their poverty.

Mr. Parker waded through ankle-deep flood water across the bridge to get to the inner city. He passed an ornate temple, the carved gods and goddesses guarding the entrance all covered with gold and elaborate decorations. The contrast between the sloppy street and the display of wealth and glitter of the exterior of the Hindu temple made a sharp declaration line separating the masses from the religious world. The building seemed to reflect the fear and reverence most Hindus have for their false gods and goddesses. Mr.Parker shook his head as he thought of how cold and impersonal the Hindu gods were.

Mr. Parker reflected on his recent meetings with the few Hindu men who had come to his Bible study. Several more had dropped out, and lately, it seemed interest was waning. Except for Venkanna.

He had not really expected Venkanna to come the evening before. The torrential rains had kept everyone under cover. It had been in the morning, while Mr. Parker was spending time in prayer

and meditation that he had gotten the urge to visit Venkanna. The missionary knew well the dictates of the castes. He knew the invisible lines that were drawn around the Dalit that no one, not even a foreigner, was to cross. Yet, he had a strong desire to see this sincere man and had decided to pay him a visit.

He was not sure if he could even find Venkanna's hut. He remembered the street where he had issued the invitation but did not know which of the hovels Venkanna lived in. Venkanna Prakasheam Gunti. At least he knew the name.

"Hello! Venkanna!"

Venkanna jumped up from his squatting position over his rice bowl. Mr. Parker! He was here, calling for him? In his haste, he upset his rice dish and turned it upside down. Pochamma immediately began scooping it off the hard-packed dirt floor.

"Oh, sir!" Venkanna bobbed his head up and down, his hands together in a prayer position. "Oh, sir! Your clothes! They are all wet!" In his distress, he wanted to offer something to cover his surprise and chagrin that the foreigner had arrived at his door.

"I had to ask three times before someone knew where you live," Mr. Parker laughed gently. "I finally found you!"

"Yes, sir," Venkanna bowed again.

"You have built this house not so long ago," Mr. Parker said, noticing the thatch still fresh looking and bound sturdily on top of the rafter poles.

"Yes sir, only five months ago we finished it."

"Is your wife at home with you?" Mr. Parker asked, noticing how uneasy Venkanna was.

"Yes, she is inside. She is recovering from the loss of our baby."

Mr. Parker nodded. "I would like to pray for you today. I know you and your wife want a living child, and I want to pray for you. When Jesus was here on earth, He said we can ask God to answer our prayers in the name of Jesus and, if you consent, I want to do that for you today."

Venkanna shifted from one leg to the other. Finally, daring to look into the eyes of his visitor, he said simply, "I would be honored to have you pray for us."

There, in the middle of one of the worst slums of India, Mr. Parker began to pray. His prayer was not long or elaborate, but he prayed in faith, asking God to bless this couple with a child.

In spite of the overcast sky and impending rains, curious neighbors were already crowding around Mr. Parker and Venkanna. The children stared open-mouthed at the white-skinned man and the adults listened to his prayer. They heard him speak to his invisible God and heard him ask God to bless this couple with a child, a child who lived.

Then, Mr. Parker nodded briefly at Venkanna. "Come again the same time next week," he welcomed. Then, he turned to the crowd. "Anyone is welcome to hear about the true and living God and His Son, Jesus Christ, who came to save all people from their sins."

Venkanna followed Mr. Parker respectfully as the missionary left his house and went down the street, the mud sucking noisily at every step.

"This is so amazing!" Venkanna said to Pochamma after he returned. "Mr. Parker came to see us! To pray for us! What kind of god does he serve that makes him willing to help us, members of the Dalit caste?" the agitated man kept asking.

"I heard his prayer," Pochamma said. "He talked to his god, Jesus!"

From that time on, Venkanna faithfully kept on attending the Bible studies, and Mr. Parker instructed the eager man with teachings from the Bible. "I so wish you could read," Mr. Parker said several months into the regular studies. "You could read the stories for yourself!"

Venkanna chuckled delightedly. "Me, a Dalit, read? Oh, that would be unheard of."

"I am serious!" Mr. Parker said. Then, looking keenly at the man in front of him, he said cautiously, "Venkanna, I am going to move my family to another place."

With a quick intake of breath, Venkanna stared at Mr. Parker. "Far away?"

With a shake of his head and a smile, Mr. Parker said, "No, even closer to your village. We have found a compound where there is a big house and enough land to build some small cottages. Could you come and help us build several shelters we need?"

Venkanna nodded and said quickly, "I could help."

"Good," Mr. Parker nodded. A plan was beginning to form in his mind.

Mr. Parker studied the intense expression on the faces of the couple who now stood inside the compound wall. It was January, and the days were pleasant and sunny and the nights almost cold. But none of the three were thinking about the weather.

"Do you realize the commitment you are making?" Mr. Parker asked kindly.

Venkanna shook his head from side to side as the Indians do to give his assent, and Pochamma responded with a soft, "Yes."

Mr. Parker nodded his head also. "I do believe you. For seven months," he looked at Venkanna, "you have been coming faithfully to the Bible studies." Then he looked at Pochamma. "Then you brought your wife, and for the next five months, you have both been learning about God and listening to His Word." With a sigh of joy, he said, "I am so glad for this day. The Spirit of the Lord is calling you into repentance and salvation."

His eyes swept the two small rooms at the far edge of the walled compound. "Venkanna, you have done well in building the huts. Daily, I saw your diligence and effort as you worked for me. I appreciate that. But you do realize that I allowed you to come and live here during the week whether you became believers in Jesus Christ or not? I don't want you to think you should take this step because you live here and are employed by me. I know it makes it easier for you to stay here rather than going back and forth every day to your village. But I don't want you to make your decision based on that. It must be much deeper than any material benefits."

Venkanna said soberly, "No, sir. I want to live for Jesus Christ, whether I live here or not. I believe He is the true God."

"I believe you," Mr. Parker said, moved by the man's answer. "On Sunday, after our services, I will spend time with you in more prayer and counseling. I pray God will richly bless you the next several days."

So it was in the year 1918 that Mr. Parker led his first converts into the Christian faith. Four weeks later, he baptized them. In honor of this event, both Venkanna and Pochamma were given new names. Mr. Parker chose the name Jakob for the newly converted man and Rachel for his wife, since all Hindu given names are forms of Hindu gods or goddesses.

Then came the festival of Makar Sankranti, both a celebration of harvest and also to honor the sun god, Surya.

"Be strong," Rachel looked at her husband as they both heard the noisy committee coming down the street towards their house. "God will help you."

Jakob nodded, but did not speak. He rose from his squatting position and went to the door of their hut. It was the weekend, and they had returned home from the compound.

From house to house, the Surya committee went, collecting the religious offering needed in preparation for the great festival the next week. Elaborate effigies of Surya and his lesser gods would be constructed from paper mache, painted and gilded and hoisted onto platforms to parade through the streets of the village. Even the Dalit were expected, as Hindus, to participate in paying their dues.

With beating of drums and shrill pipings on wind instruments, the musicians accompanied the offering collectors, making a small celebration as a prelude and helping build up excitement for the huge event. Jakob waited by his doorway, looking up into the blue sky, his lips moving in prayer.

Now, the band was only two huts away. Jakob shifted from one foot to the other. He cleared his throat.

The drummers appeared in front of the small porch shading the doorway. The Hindu priest, dressed in elaborate orange robes, carried a gilded box in front of him.

"Offering money for Surya!" He thrust the box towards Jakob.

Chapter Conclusion

What will Jakob do? What do you think the men might do if he doesn't give money for the Hindu god?

Jesus once told those who would follow Him that they must count the cost of doing so (Luke 14:27-28). It might cost them money, influence, relationships, and even physical safety, so why do it?

Do you believe that Jesus is the Son of God and that knowing Him is the greatest good?

Enduring Hope

Venkanna and Pochamma had taken on new names. Do you remember why? What were their new names?

Following Jesus means more than taking a new name though. It means worshipping Him as God alone, and that meant trouble for Jakob and Rachel when the sun god festival arrived. When we left off, the followers of Surya had held out the offering pot to Jakob and demanded that he give money to Surya. What would Jakob do? Would he turn back from following Jesus now that there was trouble?

* * * * *

Jakob slowly shook his head, "I am a Christian. I cannot pay offering money for Surya. The sun god is not alive, only an idol."

The priest looked with unbelieving eyes at first. "Gunti! I have heard about you! You have accepted the western god!"

Jakob waited without answering.

"Pay the offering! You have no choice! You are not Muslim; you are Hindu!" the priest said, referring to the large population of Muslims who lived in Hyderabad and took no part in the Hindu festivities.

"I am not Muslim. I am not Hindu. I believe in Jesus Christ, the Son of God." Jakob did not speak arrogantly, but with deep conviction.

"I have heard of you! You and your wife became Christians and were baptized by the foreigner!" He spat at the ground in front of Jakob. "You have changed your names! You are infidels! Left the gods of your ancestry and…" words seemed to fail him as he stared at Jakob, his anger increasing. "You will pay the offering!" He thrust the collection pot in front of Jakob's face and shook it.

The confrontation had drawn a crowd of onlookers. The musicians had stopped banging their drums and the wind instruments were silent as well. A hush spread out from the knot of people.

"I believe in the Lord Jesus Christ as the only true Son of God," Jakob spoke

plainly into the silence. “I refuse to pay offerings for a false god.”

A roar of incredulity rose from the collection group - a Dalit speaking like this to a Brahmin!

One of the drummers slipped the drum strap off his shoulders and moved up behind the priest. “You cannot speak to a priest like this!” A chorus of support came from the group of eight musicians.

“Pay the offering!” the priest screamed, shoving the pot against Jakob’s chest.

“I cannot,” Jakob said calmly, but his voice was drowned out by the agitated group. More of the musicians unstrapped their drums and moved in a semi-circle behind the priest.

“You will be punished,” the enraged priest shouted. “We honor Surya! The great sun god, Surya, of the Hindus!”

With clenched fists, the men pressed forward and began hitting Jakob. A slap from a brawny man hit the side of the slender victim’s face and Jakob gave a gasp of pain as his head flew to one side. The screams and disapproval of the maddened men filled the air.

Jakob was pulled out into the street and pummeled from all sides. He tried to protect his face and, as he put his hands up, he lost his balance and collapsed onto the dirt street.

Then, the attackers began kicking the hapless man, the priest egging them on with shouts of “Surya! We honor Surya! Down with the western god!”

Rachel did not dare come to the aid of her husband. But she was on her knees, praying in desperation! “God! Lord Jesus! Oh help us! Don’t let them kill my husband! Please Lord!” She could hardly think of any other words to pray, so she kept on praying, “Have mercy, oh Jesus!”

Jakob’s screams of pain rose up above the din. “Lord Jesus! Help me! Save me!”

Then, the men stopped kicking at the collapsed form. They stood around him in a circle, their breathing hard and coming with short, explosive bursts. “Come on!” the priest said with authority, motioning with his head. “We must continue collecting for Surya! We honor the sun god, the Hindu Surya who is giving us longer days and more light!" He tried to pick up a vestige of dignity and authority and the musicians picked up their drums and began their rhythmic beats.

Rachel ran out into the street as soon as the group moved on and threw herself down beside her husband. She turned his head and cried out, "Oh! Oh! Oh!" She saw his chest moving and knew he was still alive and also conscious, for he kept moaning in pain. Turning to several neighbor men who were watching, she called, "Come! Move him inside!"

The men came and helped the distraught woman. They picked up the moaning man and placed Jakob on the mat inside the hut and then left. Rachel tipped the water jug and poured water into her cupped hand and wet Jakob's lips. With a moan, the injured man licked the water on his lips gratefully.

* * * * *

Over several days and months, Jakob's wounds slowly healed. Even a year later, he still walked with a slight limp, but it did not matter to him. His suffering had been replaced by joy.

"The baby is alive!" cried the excited mid-wife. She handed the infant to her assistant and turned to Rachel. "Your baby is alive!" Outside, Jakob heard the pronouncement and raised his hands in the night toward the starry sky, and said fervently, "Thank You, Jesus!"

It was a little girl.

In Indian society boys were more highly valued than girls. Baby boys were celebrated for the wealth they would eventually bring to the family, but baby girls? They were considered a burden. They would one day require a dowry before being married.

Some of the neighbors only scoffed at the news.

"The foreigner's god gave them a girl. His god must not be very powerful."

But Jakob and Rachel rejoiced. Even if their neighbors saw the little girl as a burden to the poor couple, Jakob and Rachel knew this was God's gift to them. Didn't the Bible teach that all life was precious, whether someone was a boy or

a girl, a Dalit or a Brahmin?

Other neighbors took more notice.

"That foreigner prayed for them to have a baby that lived," the neighbors remembered. "Maybe his god is a powerful god." For the neighbors had seen the transformation of Venkanna and Pochamma into Jakob and Rachel. They had seen their fellow Dalit neighbors begin to have a purpose for living and a change in their lifestyle.

"The Gunti baby is alive!" Like a flash, the news spread throughout the slums and the women came to see the new baby.

"Jesus blessed us with this girl," Rachel told the visitors over and over.

"We will see how long she lives," more than one of the ladies said warningly.

But little Deva Karuna (meaning "God's mercy"), as they named their daughter, lived. Not only lived, but was remarkably healthy.

Mr. Parker rejoiced with the couple. When Rachel had recovered from the birth, he once again invited them to live in one of the huts in his compound.

God was blessing the little mission. No longer were Jakob and Rachel the only converts. Young people, mostly boys, were coming to Mr. Parker's Bible meetings, and when Mr. Parker had a vision to educate these youngsters, among the students was Jakob.

"I want to learn how to read," Jakob told Mr. Parker. "I want to read the Bible."

Mr. Parker nodded. "That is good, Jakob. Your desire to read the Bible will be a great boost in your learning to read." He enrolled the man in his classes.

A Dalit school? Untouchables reading? And writing? Why would the lowest caste in India need to be educated?

Yet Mr. Parker knew why. They needed to be able to read the Bible for themselves in order for them to grow in their spiritual lives. He could not always be with them.

Then, a year and a half later, Rachel delivered another child. A healthy boy they named Prakasham (meaning "radiant").

This time, ALL the neighbors took notice.

"Two children, and one a boy? My, this foreign god must be strong!" This testimony of answered prayers continued to amaze the Dalit in the slums. More and more of them began attending Bible classes.

"Another hut!" Mr. Parker came outside where Jakob was putting the last piece of tin on yet another room. More and more space was needed for housing as the school enrollment increased. As many as eight boys bunked in the rooms overnight and attended the classes during the day. Jakob and Rachel and their two children no longer returned to their weekend house, for Rachel cooked the daily rice and curry to feed the students.

"Yes, sir," Jakob said, a satisfied feeling spreading out from his heart. He loved his work here, and on Sundays, he now went into the Dalit neighborhood and spoke to the villagers about his faith in God. At first, there were not many listeners, but Jakob continued faithfully, praying for God to open the hearts of the villagers and believe in the true God and in His Son, Jesus Christ.

"Ouch!"

Jakob looked down and saw Mr. Parker lifting his one foot, his face twisted in pain.

"Oh, sir! You have injured yourself!" Jakob quickly went down off the roof and rushed over to the white man.

"I stepped on a nail! It went right through my sandal and into my foot." Mr. Parker lifted his foot and slipped the sandal off his right foot. He reached out and steadied himself against the wall of the newly constructed hut.

"You must go to the doctor!" Jakob suggested.

"No, no," Mr. Parker protested. "I will go inside and wash it off. I will get Peter to prepare a foot tub for soaking." He limped towards the house.

Jakob continued his work.

That night, Mr. Parker cancelled the Bible study. His pained foot throbbed and he slept fitfully.

By the next morning, Mr. Parker knew he needed to seek medical attention, and with his houseboy, Peter, accompanying him, he went by rickshaw to the hospital.

For two days, school was cancelled and not much was heard about their beloved Mr. Parker. The students waited and Jakob continued with his work. At least he could now read the Bible, and he spent long hours reading the Bible in Telugu.

Then news came that the injured man was transported to another hospital, this one on the other side of Hyderabad. Reports came back to the anxiously waiting community that Mr. Parker had lost consciousness. Jakob and the others prayed earnestly for the missionary, and when the news came that Mr. Parker had died, they felt the blow deeply.

There was little news, if any, after that. What would happen with the compound or Mr. Parker's funeral? Later, they learned other foreign missionaries had come, conducted a funeral service, and buried the body in a cemetery, and then left.

"What will happen to us?" Rachel asked Jakob as they received the heartbreaking news. "How will the school continue?"

The students stayed on, not knowing what else to do.

Then, help arrived in the form of two men. Two foreigners that could not speak Telugu. They used interpreters to speak to the waiting group. "We are arranging for new workers to come," they said. "We offer our sympathies to you, for we know you loved Mr. Parker very much and you will miss him greatly. Yet, we also know those of you who are believers have faith that some day you will see him in heaven. He was a very brave man and had a deep desire to see Indians trust in Jesus for salvation. We see his work was not in vain, for to find Christians here is a great delight."

Then, they gave further instructions. "For awhile, this school will be closed until the new missionaries arrive. We have prayed and God has directed two young men who will come and reopen the school."

In spite of his grieving for Mr. Parker,

Jakob felt his heart lighten.

"We will want the current caretakers to stay on to watch the house and help the new men when they come," they continued. "But for now, the students need to return to their homes."

So, the only ones left were Peter, the houseboy, and Jakob and Rachel and their two children. Some neighbors urged Jakob and Rachel to return home and to forget the foreign god.

"No, I will not turn back. I have found the words of eternal life. I will follow Jesus."

Mr. Parker was dead, the other missionaries gone, but God had not left Jakob and Rachel. He was with them! Jakob opened his Bible from which Mr. Parker had taught him to read. Jakob reminded Rachel of a promise from the Lord. He read from Hebrews 13:5, "I will never leave you, nor forsake you."

Eventually the two missionary men arrived and the school reopened. Jakob and Rachel continued to serve, and as the years passed, more children were added to their family. Other people listened to the missionaries' teaching and became Christians. Soon, a church was formed. Every Sunday, the little group would gather to worship, pray, and listen to the Bible.

People continued to harass them for their faith in Jesus, but with every harsh word, cold shoulder, and slap, the little band gained strength and refused to turn back from the faith. The church grew in strength and in number.

Many years later, thousands of children sat and listened to a man named Sam tell them about Jesus. For many of them it was the first time they'd ever heard of Jesus, the Son of God.

The man smiled as he said, "Children, I want you to know the good news of Jesus Christ. He is the Son of God. He came to this earth and died on the cross, so that you might have eternal life. This was the good news that my grandparents heard from a man named Mr. Parker. And now, I am telling you this same good news, that you might believe and have eternal life. Children, will you turn from your sin and trust in Jesus as Savior? Will you follow Jesus?"

Chapter Conclusion

That question is for you, too. Many who saw and heard Jesus when He was here on earth, yet many turned back from following Him because of unbelief or fear of what it would cost them to be His disciple. In this story, you have read the truth about who Jesus is and what He has done to provide salvation for you.

But, perhaps you are thinking the same thing as those who turned back in unbelief and fear. Will you follow Jesus?

He will help you to walk with Him your entire life long. Even when it is hard to hang on to God, He has promised to never let go of His children. Will your faith in God endure with no turning back?

Scan the QR code to find more information and videos related to this story.

REVIEW QUESTIONS

Chapter 1

1. Why were Venkanna and Pochamma gathering poles? *(To build a new house)*
2. Where did the couple live? *(India; outside the city of Hyderabad.)*
3. Where did they go for shelter when the rain started? *(To some rocks on the hillside.)*
4. How did Venkanna get water for them to drink? *(He used a jug to collect rain water.)*
5. Why had not many people come to gather wood in this place before? *(There were wild animals and snakes in the area.)*
6. What type of animal appeared among the rocks while they were sheltering there? *(A tiger.)*
7. What was one warning Venkanna gave to his wife to keep the tiger from attacking? *(don't move, don't scream, don't look it in the eye.)*
8. Even though Venkanna and Pochamma did not know the one true God at this point, what were some of the things God provided them in this chapter? *(wood, water, safety.)*

Chapter 2

1. Why were Venkanna and Pochamma grieving at the beginning of this chapter? *(Because their son had been born dead.)*
2. What did they do with their money to try to get a child? *(They offered it to the priests of the Hindu gods.)*
3. To which caste in Indian society did Venkanna and Pochamma belong? *(Dalit, "untouchables.")*
4. Why was Venkanna so surprised to see a foreigner near his home? *(He was in the slums, he spoke Telegu.)*
5. What did the man tell Venkanna about Jesus? *(That He is the Son of God; that He gives eternal life.)*
6. What did Venkanna have to give up to get some water for his wife? *(His shirt.)*
7. After Venkanna returned home, what did he decide to do? *(To go see Mr. Parker and learn more about Jesus.)*
8. Mr. Parker was a missionary to India. How did his actions remind you of Jesus? *(Answers will vary.)*

Chapter 3

1. What did Venkanna do with the pictures of the Hindu gods in his house? *(He took them down.)*
2. Why did Venkanna want a more powerful god? *(He wanted one that could provide him children.)*
3. What did Venkanna do on the way to Mr. Parker's house? Why? *(He washed in the river to try to purify himself before god.)*
4. What surprised Venkanna about the way Mr. Parker prayed? *(He spoke plainly and boldly; he thanked God for answered prayers and the gospel opportunity with the men.)*
5. Name one of the things that Mr. Parker taught Venkanna about Jesus? *(Jesus always existed; He's the Son of God; He was born of the Holy Spirit and a young girl; He performed many miracles and showed compassion and love towards others; He upset the religious rulers by His teaching; He was arrested and crucified; He rose again!)*
6. Why was Venkanna so surprised that Jesus ministered to poor people? *(In India, ruling caste people had nothing to do with people in low castes.)*
7. What did Venkanna try to do with his money after learning about Jesus? How did Mr. Parker respond? *(He tried to buy Jesus as a god for his house; Mr. Parker explained that Jesus is the living God and not for sale.)*
8. Read I Thessalonians 2:7-8. How was Mr. Parker's ministry to Venkanna and others similar to the way the Apostle Paul ministered to the people in Thessalonica? *(He shared with them the truth of the Gospel and did not get angry when Venkanna didn't understand; he gave of himself by opening his home, offering food and taking time to continue to meet with Venkanna and others.)*

Chapter 4

1. What happened to the pictures of the Hindu gods Venkanna and Pochamma had taken down? *(They were ruined by the rains.)*
2. What did Venkanna do when Mr. Parker first showed up at his house? *(Spilled his rice bowl.)*
3. What did Mr. Parker ask to do for the couple? *(To pray to God that they might have a living baby.)*
4. What did Mr. Parker ask Venkanna to do for him at the new compound? *(Build shelters.)*
5. Why did Mr. Parker want to make sure that the couple knew they could live at the compound whether they were Christians or not? *(He wanted to make sure they were not following Jesus just to get some material thing.)*
6. Four weeks after they became Christians, what did the couple do to show others they were followers of Jesus? *(They were baptized.)*
7. What new names did Mr. Parker give to Venkanna and Pochamma? Why? *(Jakob and Rachel; their old names were forms of the Hindu gods.)*
8. Why were the festival committee members going from house to house? *(To collect an offering for Surya the sun god.)*

Chapter 5

1. Why did Jakob refuse to pay the offering to Surya? *(Because it was a false god and he believed in Jesus as the One and only God now.)*
2. What happened to Jakob as a result of his refusal? *(He was beaten.)*
3. What good news did Jakob and Rachel celebrate a year later? *(The birth of a daughter.).* Why did some scoff at this news? *(Girls were not as valued as boys in Indian society.)*
4. Why did Mr. Parker encourage the Dalit people to learn to read and write? *(So they could read the Bible for themselves and grow in their faith.)*
5. How did Mr. Parker injure his foot? *(He stepped on a nail.)*
6. After Mr. Parker died, what did the two visitors tell the Christians? *(His work was not in vain; the school would close until other missionaries arrived.)*
7. What promises from God's Word did Jakob and Rachel hold on to when the others had left? *(That God would not leave them.)*
8. Who was the man who told many children about Jesus years later? *(The grandson of Jakob and Rachel.)*

No Turning Back

a salvation story of India

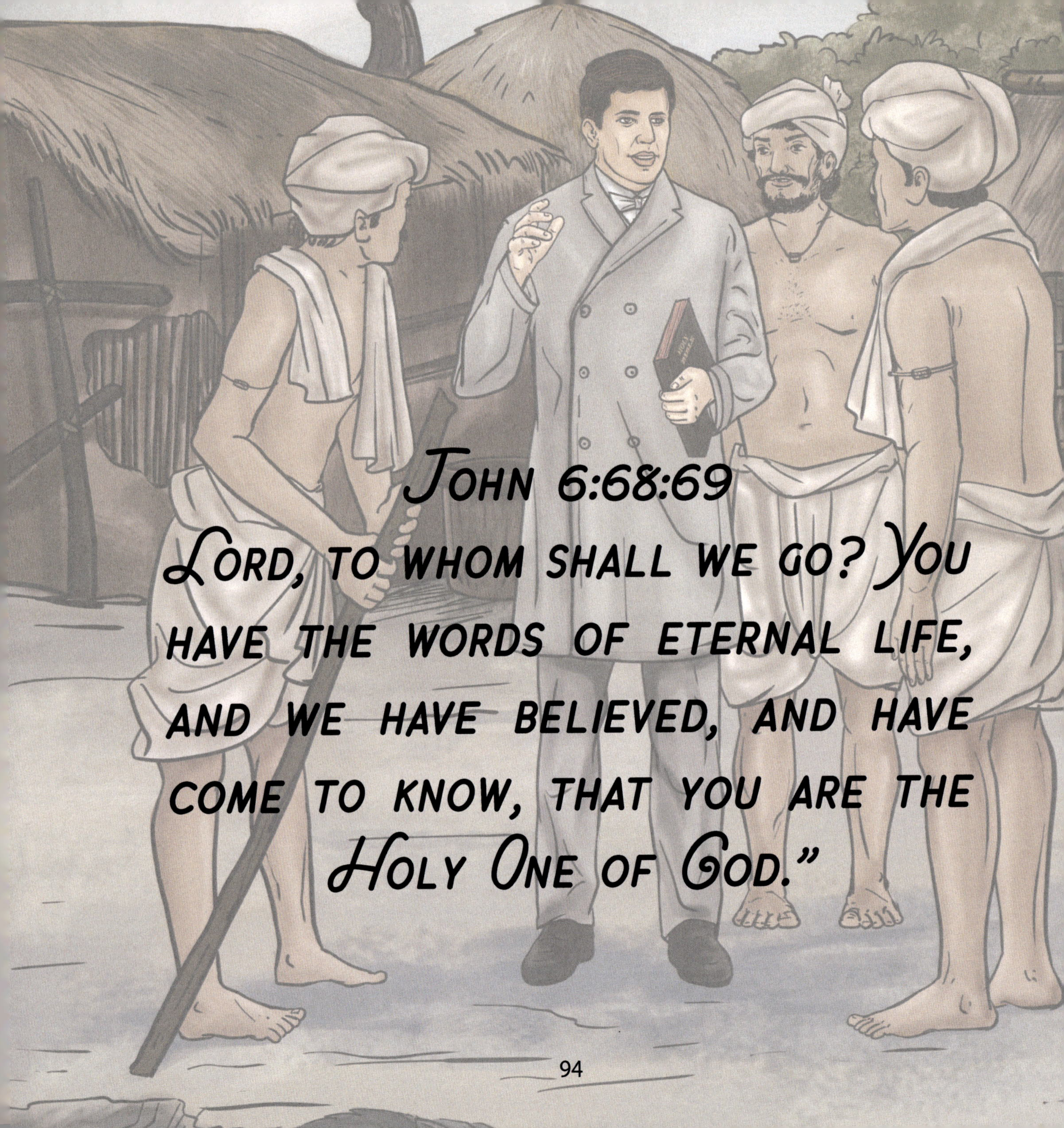
John 6:68:69
Lord, to whom shall we go? You have the words of eternal life, and we have believed, and have come to know, that you are the Holy One of God."

PAKISTAN
Himalaya Mountains
NEPAL
BHUTAN
New Delhi
Taj Mahal
Ganges River
Kolkata
INDIA
BANGLADESH
Mumbai
Hyderabad
MYANMAR
Bay of Bengal
Arabian
Sea
Chennai

The Guntis

Mr. Parker

Scan the QR code to find more information and videos related to this story.

Made in the USA
Middletown, DE
23 February 2025